NEXT
STATION
2
Amanda Cant / Mary Charrington
Sarah Elizabeth Sprague
STUDENT'S
BOOK

CB074417

FSC
www.fsc.org
MISTO
Papel produzido
a partir de
fontes responsáveis
FSC® C021887

macmillan
education

CONTENTS

LOOK AND DO / LISTEN AND DO

Activities to interpret the picture of the unit opener pages

LISTEN

Audio tracks to practice listening skills

WORLD MUSIC

Songs with a World Music flavor

TEMPLATE

Photocopiable Language File activities to use in class

 **BE** sociable and creative. Know yourself!

 **THINK** critically when you use information!

 **LEARN** to do things by yourself. Learn how to learn!

 **COLLABORATE / COMMUNICATE** with others. Teamwork is cool!

 **ACT** respectfully, be tolerant, and friendly!

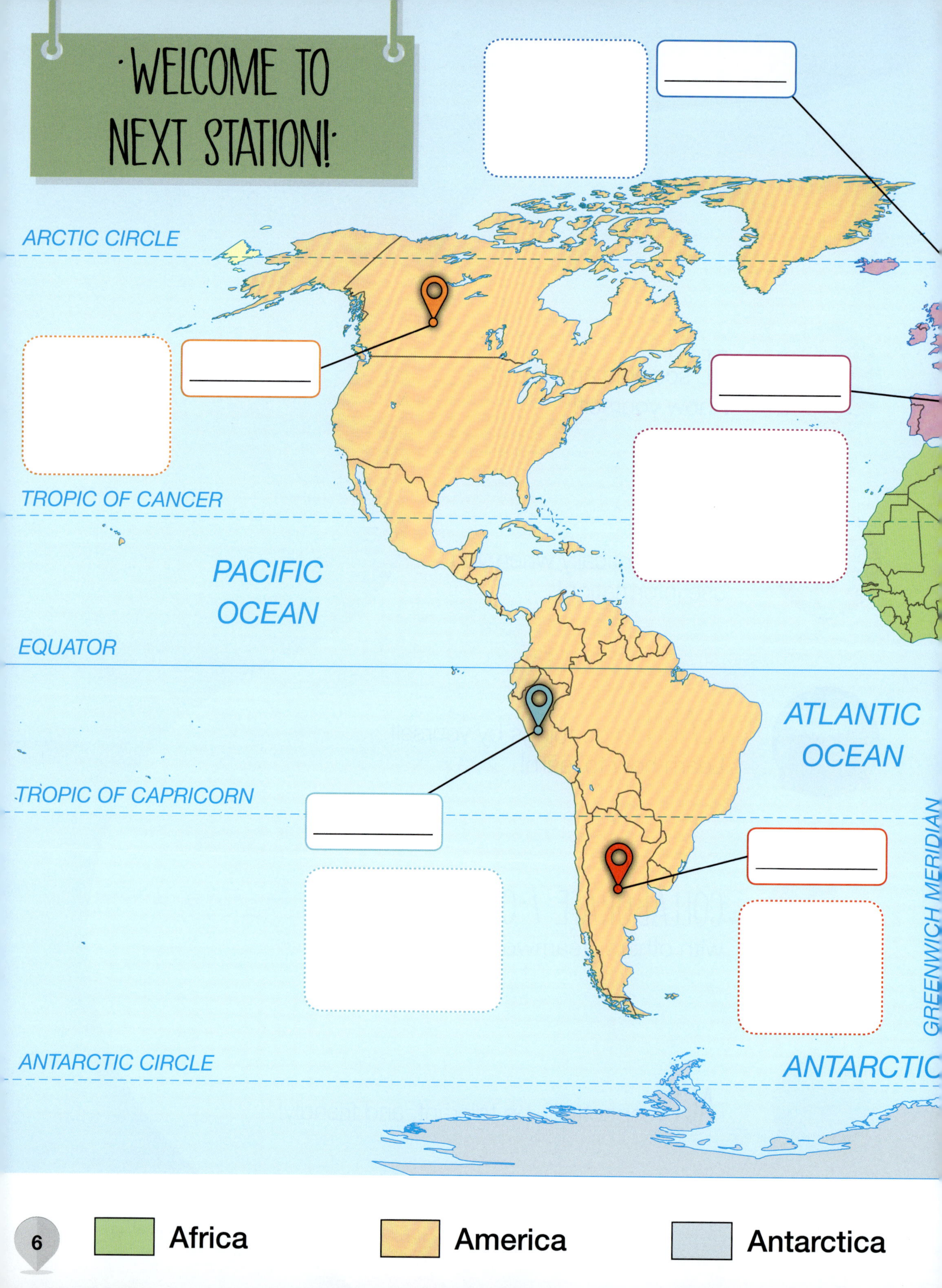
·WELCOME TO NEXT STATION!·
ARCTIC CIRCLE
TROPIC OF CANCER
PACIFIC OCEAN
EQUATOR
ATLANTIC OCEAN
TROPIC OF CAPRICORN
GREENWICH MERIDIAN
ANTARCTIC CIRCLE
ANTARCTIC
6
Africa
America
Antarctica

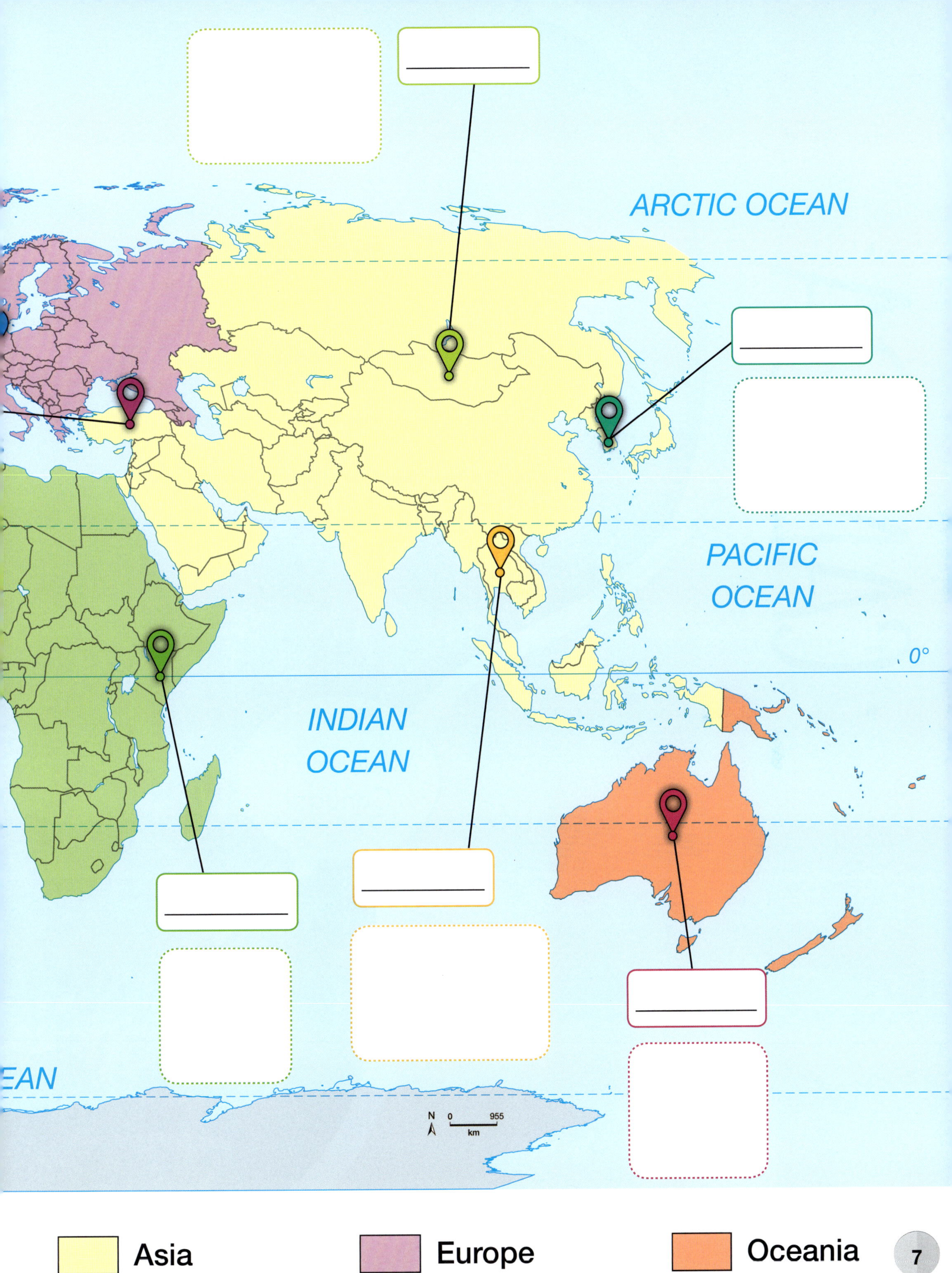

ARCTIC OCEAN
PACIFIC OCEAN
INDIAN OCEAN
0°
N
0   955
km
Asia
Europe
Oceania

CANADA
WELCOME TO
CANADA
TORONTO AIRPORT
(TIME 05:00 AM)
08 APR
ARRVL.
UNIT 1
Welcome to Canada!

Look at the picture and circle.
There are pandas / brown bears
in the mountains / towns in Canada.
Don't shout, please!

Lesson **1**

· VOCABULARY·

TRACK 2

1 Listen, point, and say.

3 talk

5 shout

1 stand up

2 sit down

4 clean up

6 run

2 Look and circle.

1 shout / clean up

2 talk / run

3 stand up / sit down

3 Play the Action Game.

WORKBOOK
page 4

TRACK 3

1 Listen, read, and say.

2 Number in order.

1 up,   please.   Clean

2 down.   Don't   sit

3 Play the Please Game.

WORKBOOK
page 5

GRAMMAR
GUIDE
page 129

TRACK 4

1 Listen and chant.

TRACK 5

2 Listen and say.

ake   ate

cake

plate

snake

lake

3 Look and write.

_____ _____ ake

_____ _____ ate

_____ ake

_____ ake

 **4** Read the chant and underline *ake* and *ate*.

·READING TIME·

1 Listen and read.

2 Read the story again. Check (✔) the **value** ⭐.

Eat fruit. ◯   Be polite. ◯

3 Circle the polite words. Do you use these words?

please / don't / thank you / sorry / cherries

Lesson 5

TRACK 7

1 Listen, point, and sing. **The ABC Song**

1 A B C D E F G

2 H I J K L M N

3 O P Q R S T U V

4 W X Y Z

2 Ask and answer.

TEMPLATE 1

3 Complete. Then write the secret words.

14

· GRAMMAR ·

How do you spell "snake"?

1 Listen, read, and say.

2 Number in order.

do ◯   spell ◯   you ◯   How ◯   "dog"? ◯

3 Ask and answer.

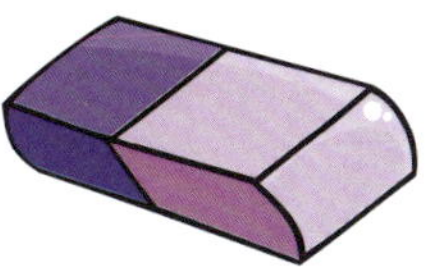
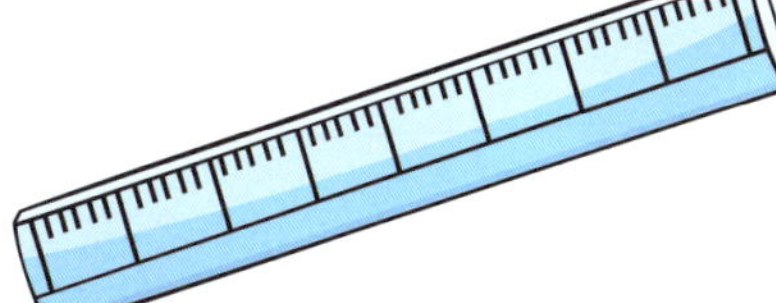

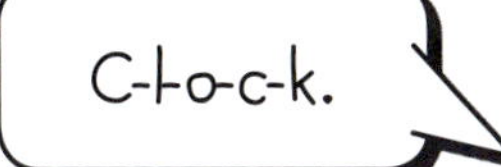

LET'S VISIT CANADA

1 Read about national favorites from Canada.

Think Twice

1 Circle.

Ice hockey / Soccer is the national sport of Canada.

The brown bear / beaver is the national animal of Canada.

2 What is the national sport of your country?

· SPEAKING TIME ·

1 Draw, write, and say.

> The national animal of Canada is a beaver.
> What's the national animal of your country?

1 Complete the conversation. Choose your response.

2 Act out the conversation.

GERMANY
ARRIVAL
GERMANY
18 AUG
BERLIN AIRPORT
Welcome to
Germany!
UNIT
2

€279,-
TRACK 9
Listen and find
the clock.
Look at the
clocks!

·VOCABULARY·

  **TRACK 10**

1 Listen, point, and say.

1 second

2 minute

3 hour

4 morning

5 afternoon

6 evening

 **TRACK 11**

2 Listen and circle.

1 15 minutes / 15 seconds

2 7 minutes / 7 hours

3 5 seconds / 5 hours

3 Look, write, and act.

1 Good

________________________.

2 Good

________________________.

3 Good

________________________.

WORKBOOK
page 11

TRACK 12

1 Listen, read, and say.

TRACK 13

2 Listen, draw, and write.

1 What time _______________?

It's _______________.

2 What _______________ is it?

_______________.

3 Make a clock. Ask and answer.

TEMPLATE 2

WORKBOOK
page 12

GRAMMAR GUIDE
page 129

·SOUNDS GREAT·

TRACK 14

1 Listen and chant.

Nine dimes in a line.
Look! One more dime.
One more time!

TRACK 15

2 Listen and say.

ime **ine**

time

dime

nine

line

3 Look and write the letters in order.

neil

tmie

ienn

eidm

4 Read the chant and underline *ime* and *ine*.

·READING TIME·

TRACK 16

1 Listen and read.

2 Read the story again. Check (✓) the **value**.

Look at the time. ◯   Don't be late. ◯

3 How do you feel when you are late? Circle.

Lesson 5

· VOCABULARY·

TRACK 17

1 Listen, point, and say.

1 get up

2 have breakfast

3 go to school

4 have lunch

5 have dinner

6 go to sleep

TRACK 18

2 Listen and say what's next.

TRACK 19

3 Sing and act. **My Busy Day**

I get up and I have breakfast,
At the start of every day.
I go to school and I have lunch,
I work and then I play.
I have dinner with my family.
Then I have time to play.
I go to bed and I go to sleep.
It's a busy, busy, day!

WORKBOOK
page 15

TRACK 20

1 Listen, read, and say.

2 Complete about you.

1 I have breakfast at _______________________ o'clock.

2 _______________________ go to school at _______________________.

3 _______________________ have dinner at _______________________.

3 Play the Mime Game.

WORKBOOK
page 16

GRAMMAR GUIDE
page 129

LET'S VISIT GERMANY

1 Read about traditional food from Germany.

Look at this! It's a traditional German chocolate cake! It's called Black Forest cake. It has chocolate, cream, and cherries. It's delicious. I eat chocolate cake in the afternoon and evening! Is it time for cake?

Think Twice

1 Read and check (✓).

Black Forest cake has chocolate, ◯

cream, ◯ trees, ◯

cherries, ◯ pears. ◯

2 When do you eat cake?

1 Draw, write, and say.

NEW FRIENDS

1 Complete the conversation. Choose your response.

2 Act out the conversation.

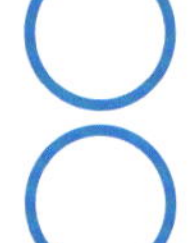

1 Read, look, and write the numbers.

1 Clean up, please.   **2** Sit down, please.   **3** Don't talk.   **4** Don't run.

2 Look, say, and write.

 **1** ________________

 **3** ________________

 **2** ________________

 **4** ________________

THINK AGAIN!

An animal from Canada is the ________________________________.

My favorite lesson is on page ________________________________.

The national sport of Canada is ________________________________.

WORKBOOK page 18   STICKERS   PASSPORT page 2

·PROGRESS CHECK·

1 Read and draw.

1 It's three o'clock.

2 It's eight o'clock.

2 Look and write.

1 It's

_______________________.

2 It's

_______________________.

3 Look and complete.

THINK AGAIN!

A famous food in Germany is _______________.

My favorite picture is on page _______________.

A traditional object from Germany is _______________.

WORKBOOK
page 19

STICKERS

PASSPORT
page 4

The Peace Tower clock in Ottawa, Canada.

Mythical figures adorn the building.

Gargoyles are decorative and help keep rain water away.

STEAM

TEAM NAME

Why do we need to know the time?

1 Get materials.

play dough

toothpicks

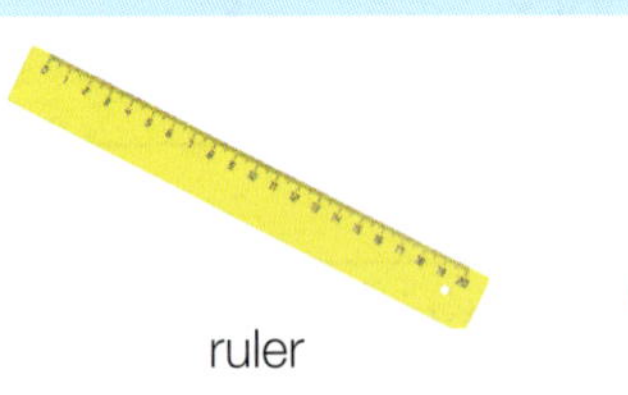
ruler

colored pencils

scissors

glue stick

paper

A clock tower has one or more clock faces.

The Peace Tower clock was a gift from the UK in 1927.

The clock of the New Town Hall was first heard in 1908.

·BUILD A CLOCK TOWER·

GERMANY

2 Look at the geometric shapes below. Draw your plan.

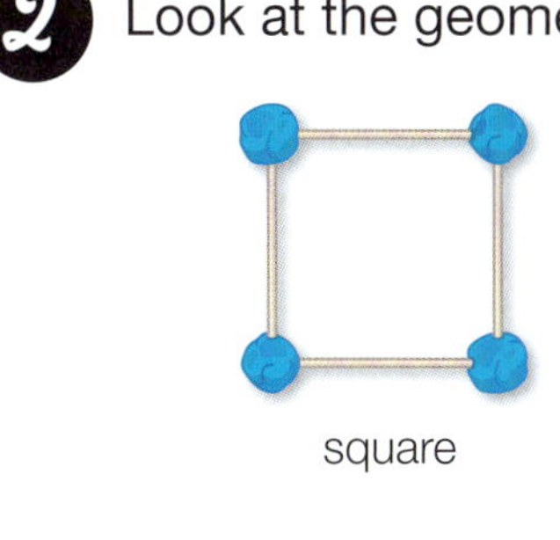

square

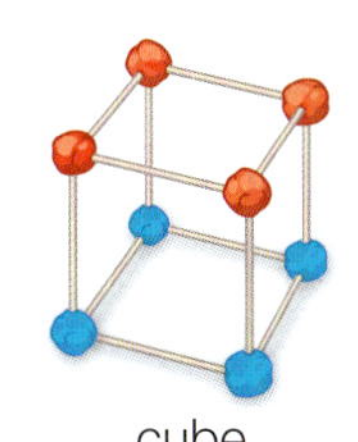

cube

triangle

tetrahedron

3 Build a clock tower.

The clock tower of the New Town Hall in Munich, Germany.

The Glockenspiel, a tourist attraction at the New Town Hall.

4 Name your clock tower.

____

5 How tall is it?

________________ cm

Did your clock tower match your drawing? Why or why not?

Some of the 32 figures on the Glockenspiel stage.

 TEAMWORK ★ ★ ★ ★ ★

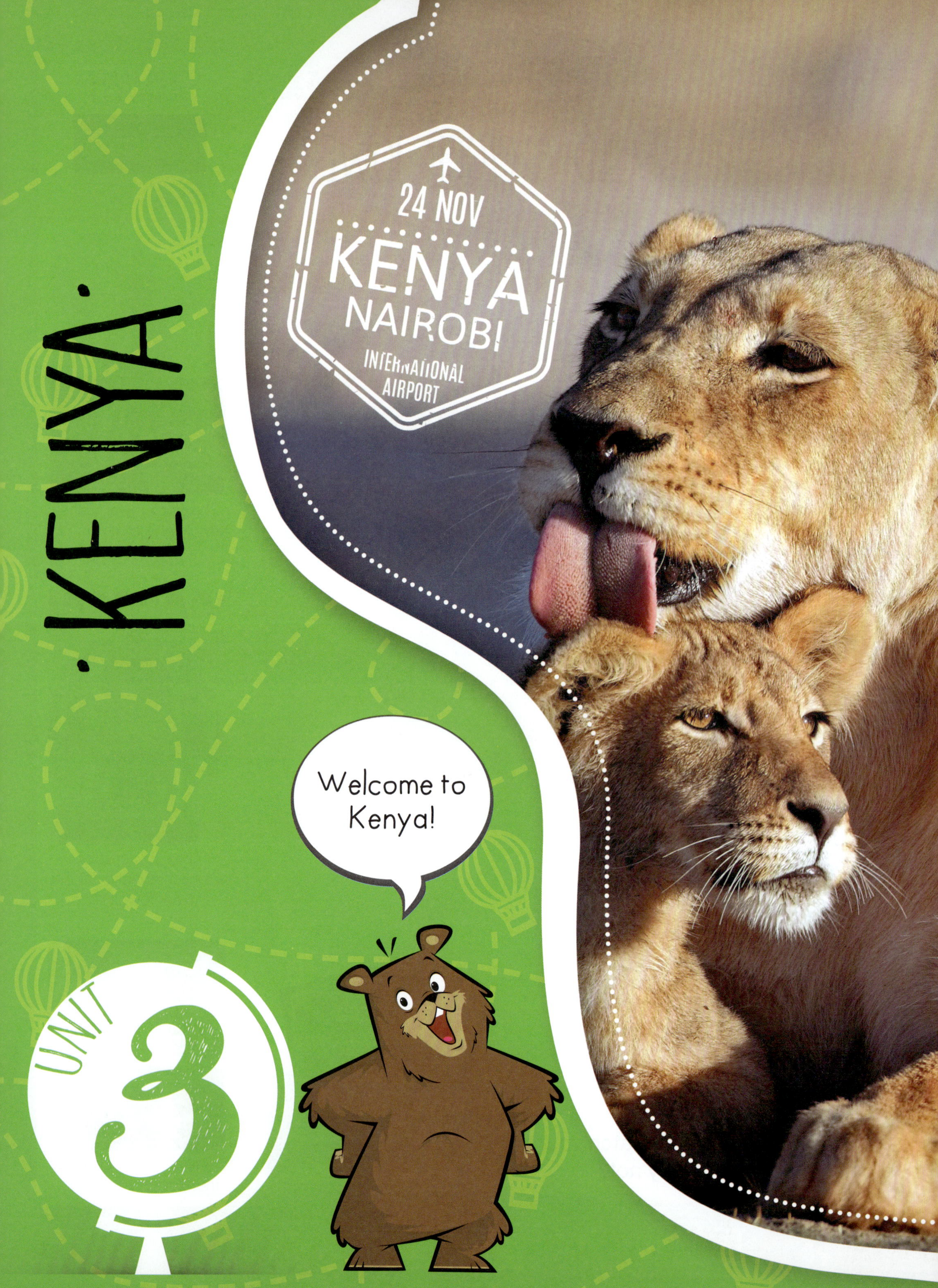
KENYA
24 NOV
KENYA
NAIROBI
INTERNATIONAL
AIRPORT
Welcome to
Kenya!
UNIT
3

Look! There are three lions.
Circle the three animals from Kenya.
1
2
3
4

·VOCABULARY·

TRACK 21

1 Listen, point, and say.

TRACK 22

2 Listen and guess.

3 Look and complete.

1 It's a _______________________.

2 It's a _______________________.

3 It's a _______________________.

4 It's a _______________________.

WORKBOOK
page 20

TRACK 23

1 Listen, read, and say.

2 Look and circle.

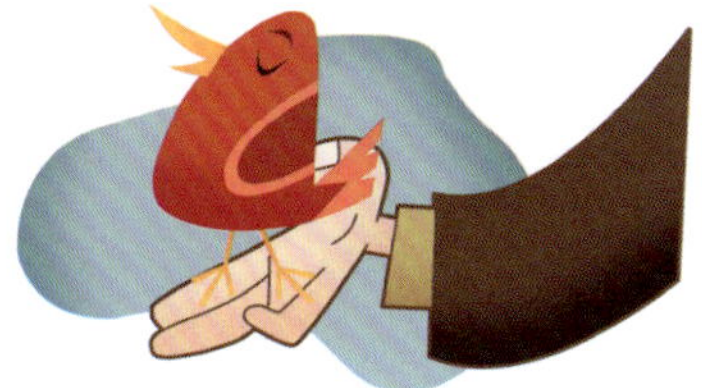

1 This is / **That's** a bird.

2 These / **Those** are chickens.

TEMPLATE 3

3 Draw and talk about your animals.

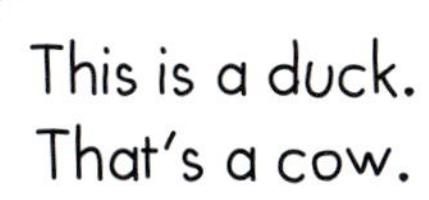

WORKBOOK
page 21

GRAMMAR
GUIDE
page 130

·SOUNDS GREAT·

TRACK 24

1 Listen and chant.

> The bone is under a stone but his nose is in a rose!

TRACK 25

2 Listen and say.

 **one**    **ose**

bone

stone

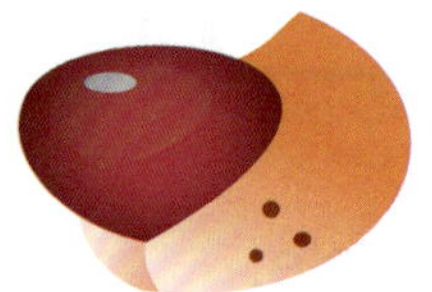

nose

rose

3 Connect and write.

1  s  t  o  n e _______________

2 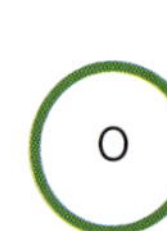 n  o  s e _______________

3  r  o  s 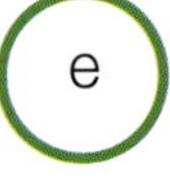 e _______________

4  b 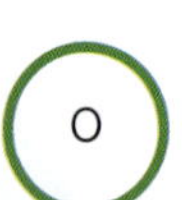 o  n  e _______________

 **4** Read the chant and underline *one* and *ose*.

·READING TIME·

1 Listen and read.

1

2

3

4

2 Read the story again. Check (✔) the **value** ⭐.

Be responsible. ◯   Listen to your grandma. ◯

3 What responsible things do you do? Circle.

WORKBOOK
page 23

·VOCABULARY·

TRACK 27

1 Listen, point, and say.

1 ladybug

2 grasshopper

3 caterpillar

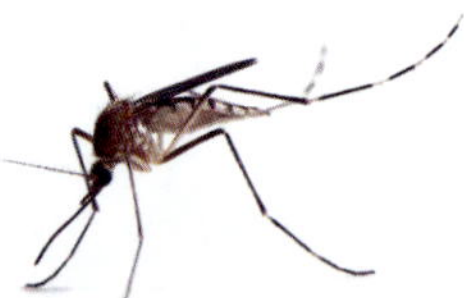
4 mosquito

5 butterfly

6 ant

 **2** Look and write.

1 These are ___________________.

2 This is a ___________________.

3 ___________________.

4 ___________________.

TRACK 28

1 Listen, read, and say.

TRACK 29

2 Sing. **Itchy, Ouchy Mosquito**

What are these? What are these?
They're green grasshoppers.
What are those? What are those?
They're curly caterpillars.

What's that? What's that?
It's a shiny black cat.
And what's this? Ooh! Ouch! Stop! Oh, no!
It's an itchy, ouchy, itchy, ouchy mosquito!

WORKBOOK page 25

GRAMMAR GUIDE page 130

LET'S VISIT KENYA

1 Read about animals in Kenya.

Kenya is famous for its animals. There are many different animals there. These are zebras. They're black and white. They are very similar to donkeys and horses.

Look at those giraffes! Wow! Their necks are long! Giraffes eat green leaves from trees for breakfast, lunch, and dinner! They love leaves.

What are these? They're birds! Pink birds! And they are called pink flamingos. They are very, very beautiful!

Think Twice

1 Read and write *z* (zebra), *g* (giraffe), or *f* (flamingo).

It's a bird. ◯ It's black and white. ◯

It has a long neck. ◯

2 Are there pink flamingos in your country?

1 Draw, write, and say.

This is a giraffe from Kenya.

This is a / an _________________
from my country.

NEW FRIENDS

1 Complete the conversation.

2 Act out the conversation.

·TURKEY·

These desserts are delicious!
Check (✓) three things from Turkey.
1
2
3
4

TRACK 30

1 Listen, point, and say.

1 peppers

2 potatoes

3 onions

4 carrots

5 beans

6 tomatoes

2 Count and write.

1   There are three peppers. ____________.

2   ____________________________.

3   ____________________________.

4   ____________________________.

5   ____________________________.

6   ____________________________.

3 Ask and answer.

1 Listen, read, and say.

2 Complete and color your answer.

	Yes, I do.	No, I don't.
1 ____Do you like____ onions?	◯	◯
2 __________ peppers?	◯	◯
3 __________ beans?	◯	◯
4 __________ potatoes?	◯	◯
5 __________ tomatoes?	◯	◯

3 Ask and answer.

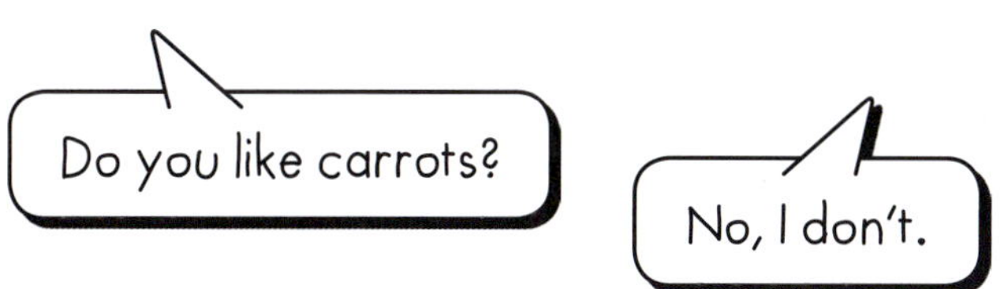

Lesson 3

TRACK 32

1 Listen and chant.

The boy plays a tune,
Under the moon.
And the girl eats prunes
With her spoon.

TRACK 33

2 Listen, say, and color.

 une  oon

spoon

prune

moon

tune

3 Write and match.

oon   une

sp ___ ___ ___

t ___ ___ ___

m ___ ___ ___

pr ___ ___ ___

4 Read the chant and underline *une* and *oon*.

·READING TIME·

1 Listen and read.

2 Read the story again. Check (✓) the **value**⭐.

Say "Thank you." ◯   Try new things. ◯

3 Look at the story and answer.

Do you try new things when you eat outside your house?

Do you like to try things that look unusual?

·VOCABULARY·

TRACK 35 

1 Listen, point, and say.

2 Match.

ice pops
French fries
sandwiches
pancakes
hamburgers
cookies

T TEMPLATE 4

3 Write. Then ask and answer.

WORKBOOK
page 31

TRACK 36

1 Listen, read, and say.

2 Talk to a friend.

beans	carrots	cookies
French fries	hamburgers	ice pops
onions	pancakes	peppers

TRACK 37

3 Sing. **I Like Food!**

Do you like hamburgers?
Yes, I do. Yes, I do.
I like hamburgers with onions.

Do you like bananas?
Yes, I do. Yes, I do.
I like bananas with hot pancakes.

Do you like everything?
No, I don't. No, I don't.
I don't like spiders and I don't like snakes!

UNIT 4

LET'S VISIT TURKEY

1 Read about food markets in Turkey.

Look at his vegetable stand. There are peppers, beans, and tomatoes.

This is a traditional market in Turkey. There are many different foods here. And they are all fresh and delicious. Don't forget, eat lots of fresh vegetables!

This is a famous candy from Turkey. It's called Turkish delight. It's very sweet! And look at all the colors! Turkish delight is yellow, orange, or green!

Think Twice

1 What can you buy at the market? Circle.

cookies / beans / French fries / peppers / ice pops / tomatoes

2 Is there a similar type of food market in your town?

· SPEAKING TIME ·

1 Draw, write, and say.

_______________________________ is a famous candy from my country.

NEW FRIENDS

1 Complete the conversation. Choose your response.

2 Act out the conversation.

1 Look, read, and number.

That's a monkey. (1)   Those are elephants. ( )   This is a ladybug. ( )

These are snakes. ( )   That's a butterfly. ( )   These are caterpillars. ( )

2 Look and write.

~~What's this?~~   What's that?   What are these?   What are those?

1 What's this? _________________________ It's a ladybug.

2 _________________________ They're caterpillars.

3 _________________________ They're elephants.

4 _________________________ It's a monkey.

THINK AGAIN!

Two animals from Kenya are ________________ and ________________.

My favorite lesson is on page ________________.

Giraffes love to eat ________________.

WORKBOOK page 34   STICKERS   PASSPORT page 6

· PROGRESS CHECK ·

1 Complete and answer *Yes, I do.* or *No, I don't.*

1 Do you like ________________? ________________.

2 Do you like ________________? ________________.

3 Do you like ________________? ________________.

4 Do you like ________________? ________________.

5 Do you like ________________? ________________.

2 Look and write.

1 I like tomatoes.   I don't like onions.

2 ________________   ________________

3 ________________   ________________

THINK AGAIN!

Two types of food from Turkey are ________________ and ________________.

My favorite picture is on page ________________.

A traditional object from Turkey is ________________.

The arid region below Mount Kenya.

Samburo child in traditional clothing.

Camel in the Chalbi desert, Kenya.

STEAM

TEAM NAME

How many minutes does it take a camel to drink 113 liters of water? 13, 23, or 30?

1 Get materials.

paper squares

measuring cup with water

Dromedary camels have only one hump. The hump is full of fat.

Bactrian camels have two humps.

Camels can go 6 months without food or water.
Their habitat is hot, dry, and sandy.

· DESIGN A PAPER CUP ·

TURKEY

2 Design a paper cup. Follow the model.

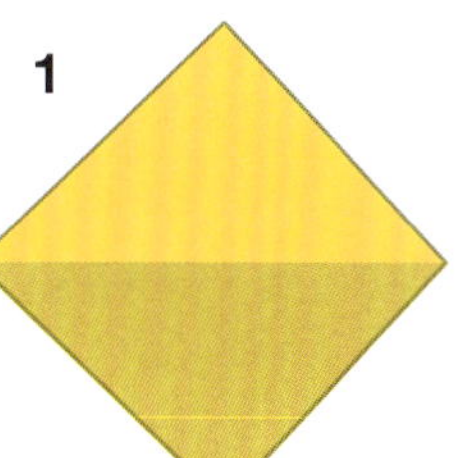
1

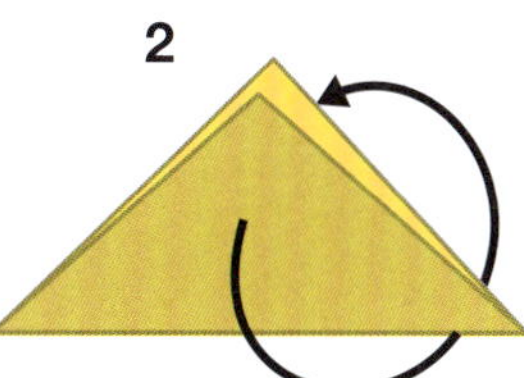
2

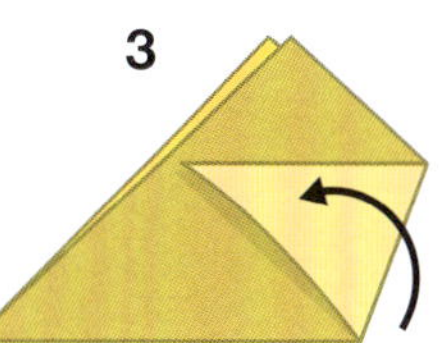
3

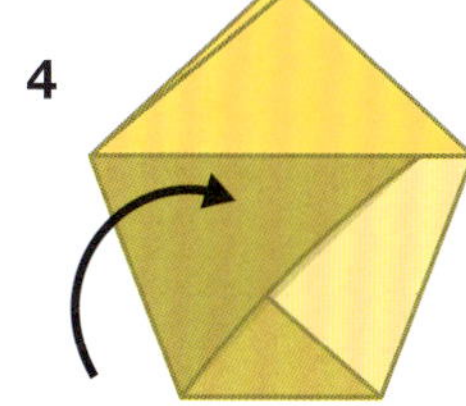
4

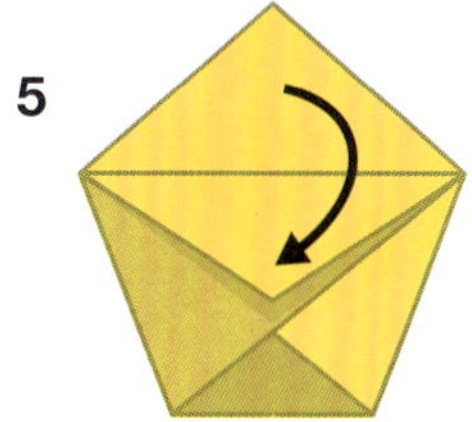
5

6

7

The semi-arid region of Cappadocia, in Turkey.

3 Fill it with water. Test your cup for 10 seconds.

How do you conserve water?

Turkish dancer in traditional clothing.

Camel with a child in Antalya, Turkey.

SOUTH KOREA
WELCOME TO
SOUTH KOREA
WELCOME TO
WELCOME TO
Welcome to South Korea!
UNIT
5

TRACK 38
Listen and circle the music from South Korea.
1
2
3
Look at her drum!

Lesson 1

TRACK 39

1 Listen, point, and say.

2 Match and say.

do	rope
play	your toes
speak	the guitar
climb	a tree
touch	Vietnamese
jump	taekwondo

3 Play the Whisper Game.

WORKBOOK
page 36

TRACK 40

1 Listen, read, and say.

2 Write.

1 Can you speak English? _______________________________.

2 Can you climb a tree? _______________________________.

3 Can you do taekwondo? _______________________________.

4 Can you play the guitar? _______________________________.

5 Can you jump rope? _______________________________.

3 Ask and answer.

Lesson 3

·SOUNDS GREAT·

TRACK 41

1 Listen and chant.

The teacher is under
A big, green tree.
"This is a bean.
Repeat after me!"

TRACK 42

2 Listen, say, and color.

ea

ee

green

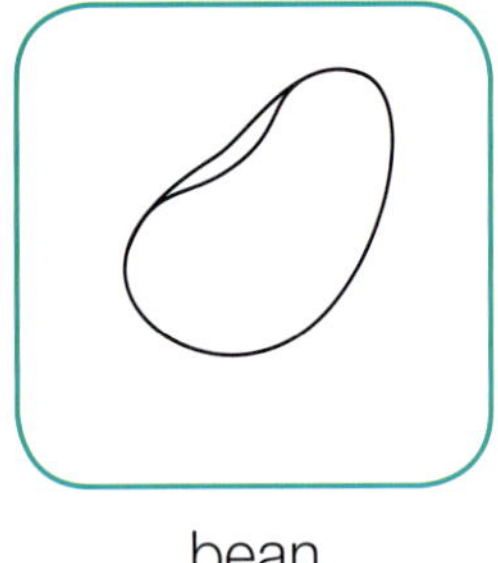

bean

teacher

tree

3 Write and match.

ea

ee

t _____ _____ cher

gr _____ _____ n

b _____ _____ n

tr _____ _____

4 Read the chant and underline *ea* and *ee*.

Lesson 4

TRACK 43

1 Listen and read.

 **2** Read the story again. Check (✓) the **value** ⭐.

Play music. ◯   Be positive. ◯

 **3** What do you say when you are being positive?

No, I can't. ◯   Yes, I can. ◯

·VOCABULARY·

TRACK 44

1 Listen, point, and say.

1 fly

2 swim

3 hop

4 sing

5 walk

6 ride a horse

2 Read and circle.

1 Can you swim?　　　　Yes, I can. / No, I can't.

2 Can you hop?　　　　Yes, I can. / No, I can't.

3 Can you walk?　　　　Yes, I can. / No, I can't.

4 Can you fly?　　　　Yes, I can. / No, I can't.

5 Can you ride a horse?　　　Yes, I can. / No, I can't.

6 Can you sing?　　　　Yes, I can. / No, I can't.

TEMPLATE 5

3 Complete the quiz. Ask and answer.

TRACK 45

1 Listen, read, and say.

TRACK 46

2 Sing and act. **I Can Do It!**

I can speak Vietnamese,
I can do taekwondo.
I can swim, I can hop,
I can touch my big toe.

I can play the guitar,
I can jump up high.
But I can't, no, I can't,
I just can't fly!

UNIT 5

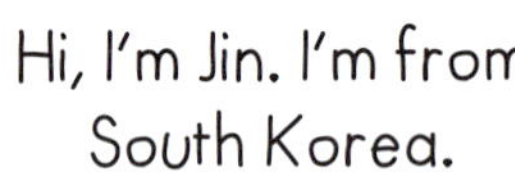

LET'S VISIT SOUTH KOREA

1 Read about special events in South Korea.

There are lots of festivals in South Korea. At the Moon Festival, some people play traditional games and eat special foods! People eat rice with nuts and beans. Do you like beans?

Dano is a Korean holiday. People sing traditional songs. They play drums and trumpets. They dance and play traditional games. And they wrestle! Can you wrestle?

Think Twice

1 Read and circle.

People eat special food at the Moon Festival.   True / False

People play guitars on the Dano holiday.   True / False

2 Can you name a special event in your country?

Lesson **8** · SPEAKING TIME·

1 Draw, write, and say.

> At festivals in my country, people eat / play
> ___________________________________.

NEW FRIENDS

1 Complete the conversation. Choose your response.

2 Act out the conversation.

ARGENTINA
CONTROL DEPARTURE
ARGENTINA
★ 25 JULY ★
approved
We're in Argentina!
UNIT
6

We like dancing!
Check (✔) three activities from Argentina.
1
2
3
4

· VOCABULARY·

TRACK 47

1 Listen, point, and say.

1 play soccer

2 watch TV

3 sing karaoke

4 play computer games

5 read books

6 play board games

TRACK 48

2 Listen and guess.

3 Check (✔) the activities in the pictures.

1 sing karaoke ◯

2 play soccer ◯

3 watch TV ◯

4 play board games ◯

5 read books ◯

6 play computer games ◯

WORKBOOK
page 43

TRACK 49

1 Listen, read, and say.

2 Look and complete.

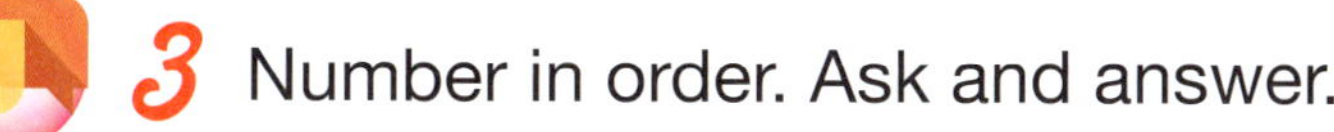

I ______don't like______ watching TV.

I __________________ playing board games.

I __________________ reading books.

I __________________ singing karaoke.

3 Number in order. Ask and answer.

you ◯   What ①   do ◯   doing? ◯   like ◯

I like playing board games.

·SOUNDS GREAT·

TRACK 50

1 Listen and chant.

It's rainy today.
Let's play a game.
Sit down with me.
Let's make a train!

TRACK 51

2 Listen, say, and color.

ai **ay**

rainy   play   train   today

3 Look and write.

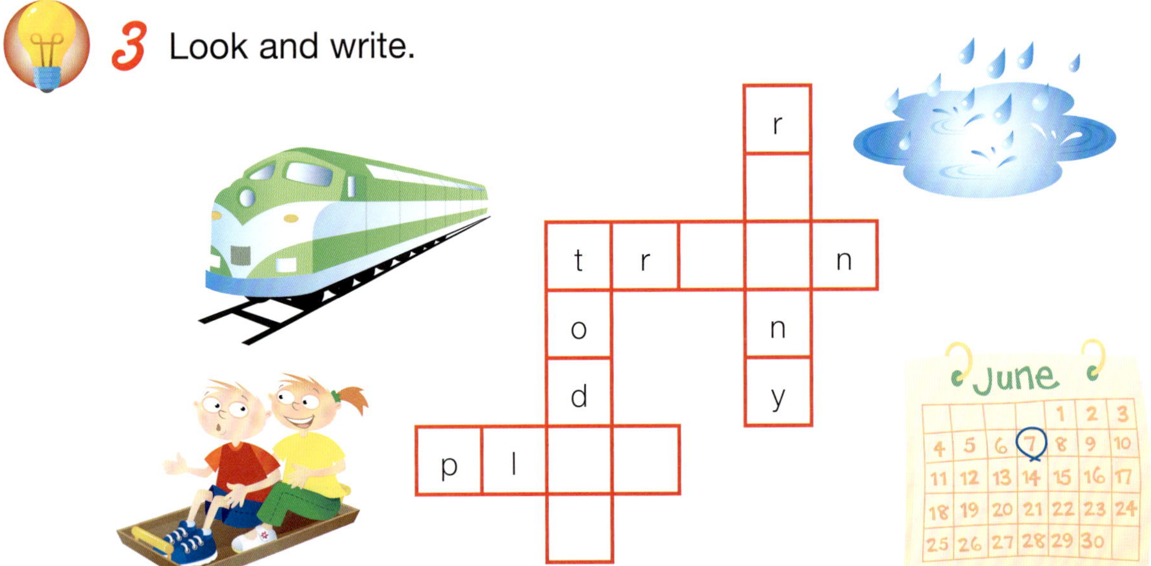

		r	
t	r		n
o		n	
d		y	
p	l		

4 Read the chant and underline *ai* and *ay*.

 **WORKBOOK** page 45

Lesson 4

TRACK 52

1 Listen and read.

2 Read the story again. Check (✓) the **value** ⭐.

Value your friends. ◯   Play outdoors. ◯

3 What do you like doing with your friends?

reading ◯   playing soccer ◯   playing games ◯   watching TV ◯

Lesson 5

· VOCABULARY ·

TRACK 53

1 Listen, point, and say.

TRACK 54

2 Listen and write their names.

3 Complete, write, and say.

WORKBOOK
page 47

GRAMMAR

He / She likes read**ing**.
He / She doesn't like sing**ing**.

1 Listen, read, and say.

2 Look and circle.

1 Bubba doesn't like singing.   True / False

2 Niki likes listening to music.   True / False

3 Sing and act. **Playing with Friends**

He likes reading books at school.
She likes swimming in the pool.

But they both like playing with friends.
They both like playing with friends.

She doesn't like climbing a tree.
He doesn't like watching TV.

Chorus

WORKBOOK page 48

GRAMMAR GUIDE page 131

LET'S VISIT ARGENTINA

1 Read about a family from Argentina.

I like playing soccer. Soccer is very popular in Argentina. We love playing soccer and watching it on TV.

This is my grandmother and grandfather. My grandma's name is Flora, and my grandpa's name is Miguel. My grandma doesn't like playing soccer! But she likes listening to music, and she likes dancing the tango. It's her favorite dance.

Think Twice

1 Circle.

Flora likes playing soccer / listening to music / dancing.

2 Do you like dancing?

·SPEAKING TIME·

1 Draw, write, and say.

NEW FRIENDS

1 Complete the conversation. Choose your response.

2 Act out the conversation.

1 Look and write. Ask and answer.

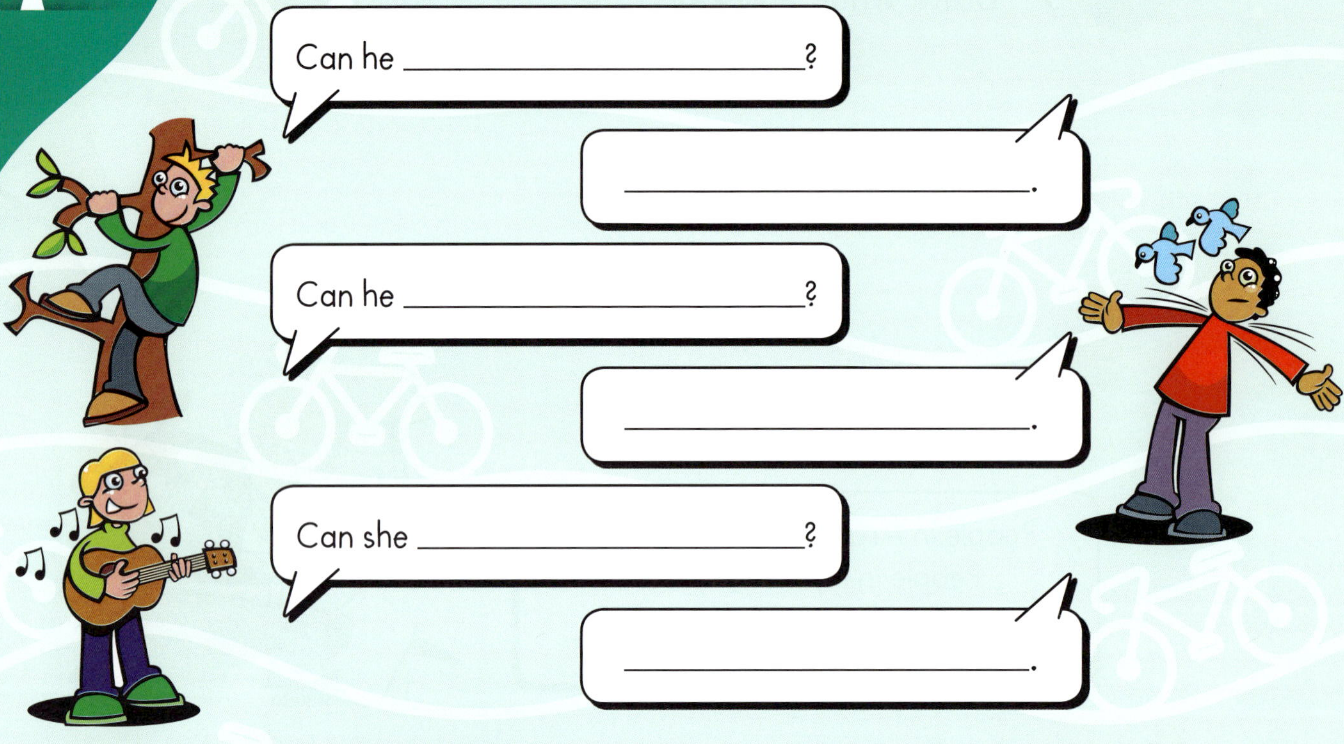

2 Write *can* or *can't*.

1 Dogs _____________ do taekwondo.

2 Ducks _____________ swim.

3 Donkeys _____________ play the guitar.

4 Snakes _____________ fly.

5 Grasshoppers _____________ hop.

6 Cats _____________ climb trees.

THINK AGAIN!

People eat _____________ and _____________ in South Korea.

My favorite lesson is on page _____________.

A musical instrument popular in South Korea is _____________.

STICKERS

1 Look and write.

I like playing board games.

____

____

____

____

____

2 Match.

He likes

She likes

She likes

listening to music.

watching TV.

drawing.

making models.

painting.

reading books.

He likes

She likes

He likes

THINK AGAIN!

A dance from Argentina is ___________________________________.

My favorite picture is on page ___________________________________.

A popular activity in Argentina is ___________________________________.

Janggu, a traditional Korean drum.

The *janggu* drum in a performance by a South Korean group.

Folk dancers with a *sogo* drum.

STEAM

TEAM NAME

What is sound? How does it travel?

1 Get materials.

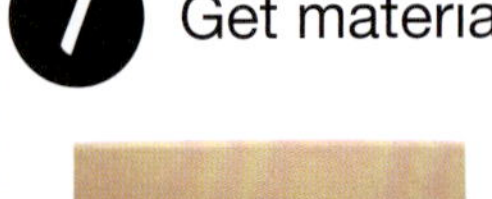
cardboard

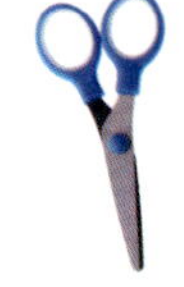
scissors

2 pieces of string

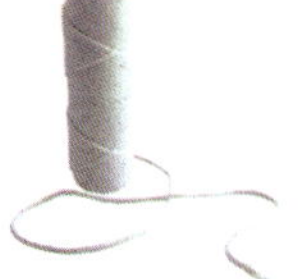
wooden stick

4 beads

markers

tape

2 Draw a cardboard circle. Cut it out.

A drum is a percussion instrument. It makes sound when hit. Drums can be very different in size and shape.

Korean CheonGo drum

djembe drum

spinning drum

· MAKE A SPINNING DRUM·

ARGENTINA

3 Ask an adult to make 2 small holes.

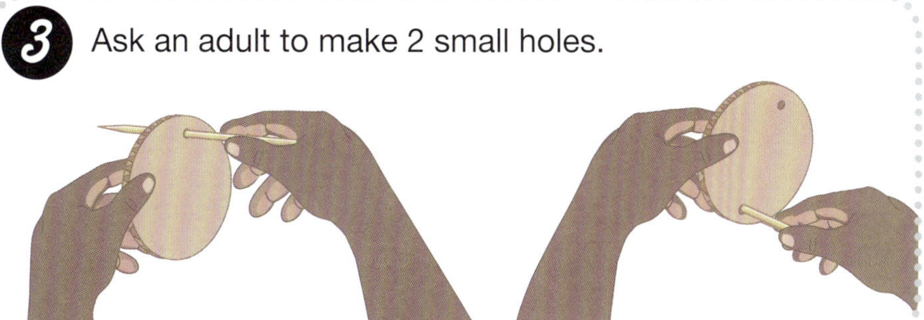

Bombo legüero, a traditional drum from Argentina.

4 Add strings and beads.

5 Insert the stick into the cardboard circle and decorate.

The *bombo legüero* in an opening festival in Argentina.

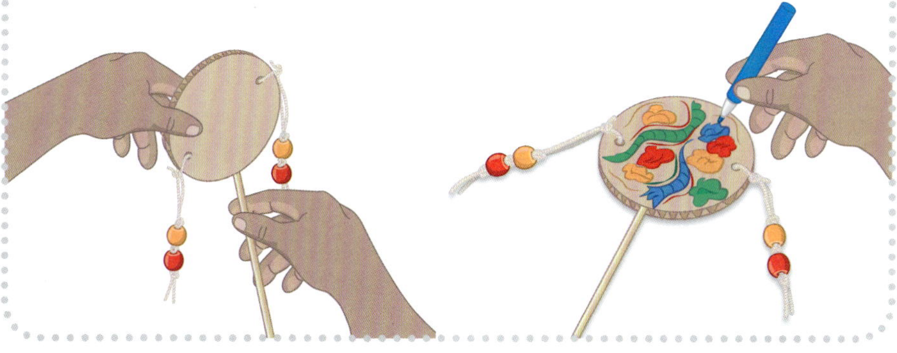

6 Test your drum.

What kind of drum is traditional in your culture? How is it played?

A folk dance accompanied by *bombo legüero*.

TEAMWORK ★ ★ ★ ★ ★

MONGOLIA

WELCOME TO
MONGOLIA
INTERNATIONAL AIRPORT
TOURISM
23 SEPT

Welcome to
Mongolia!

UNIT
7

SECURITY
Which animal doesn't
live in Mongolia?
Check (✓).
1
2
3
4

TRACK 57

1 Listen, point, and say.

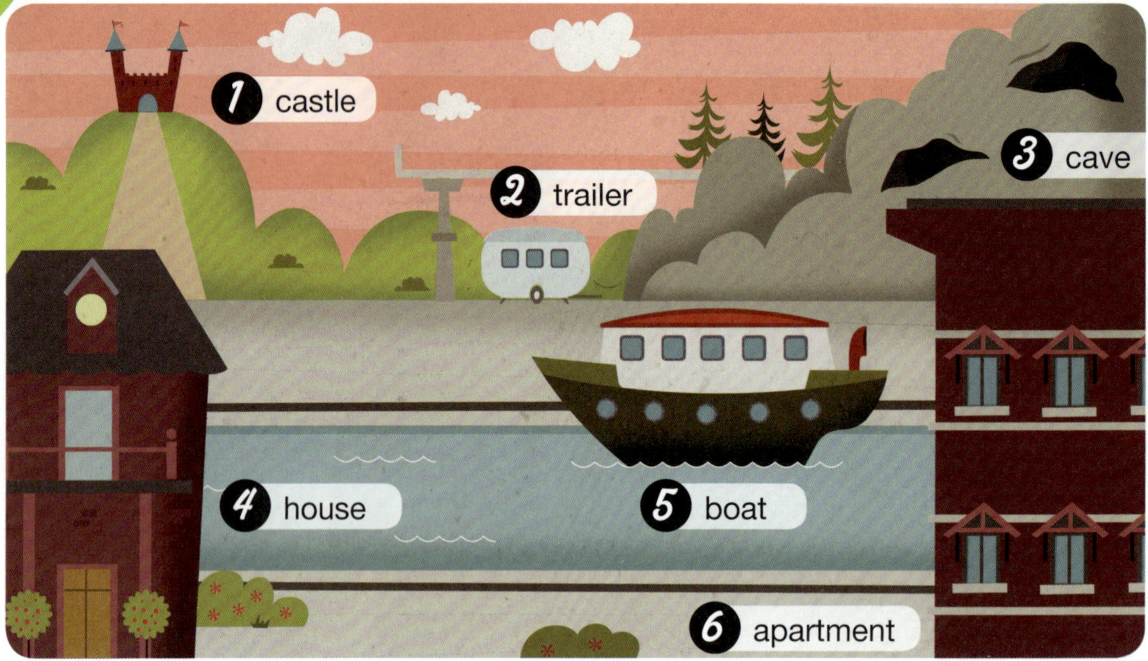

TRACK 58

2 Listen and say what's missing.

3 Draw your home and write.

This is _______________________________.

WORKBOOK
page 52

· GRAMMAR ·

He / She / It lives in a house.

TRACK 59

1 Listen, read, and say.

2 Play the Card Game.

TEMPLATE 7

WORKBOOK
page 53

GRAMMAR
GUIDE
page 132

·SOUNDS GREAT·

TRACK 60

1 Listen and chant.

The birds fly high in the sky.
The birds love apple pie.

TRACK 61

2 Listen, say, and color.

igh   y   ie

pie   sky   fly   high

3 Write and match.

p _____ _____   h _____ _____ _____   sk _____   fl _____

 **4** Read the chant and underline *igh, y,* and *ie.*

WORKBOOK
page 54

TRACK 62

1 Listen and read.

2 Read the story again. Check (✔) the **value** ⭐.

Welcome people. ◯   Talk to your neighbors. ◯

3 What do you say to a new boy or girl in your class? Circle.

Come and play with us. / Do you like spiders?

·VOCABULARY·

TRACK 63

1 Listen, point, and say.

1 ocean

2 desert

3 jungle

4 woods

5 city

6 country

2 Find and circle.

n	w	e	l	t	q	i	f	c	s	a	o	l	n	w
c	o	u	n	t	r	y	g	i	n	e	c	v	p	i
a	o	z	c	y	m	c	s	t	g	k	e	i	j	o
f	d	e	s	e	r	t	b	y	c	f	a	u	m	p
m	s	p	d	m	s	e	l	h	j	u	n	g	l	e

3 Complete.

1 The iguana lives in the _______________________________.

2 The bird lives in the _______________________________.

3 The bear lives in the _______________________________.

4 The fish lives in the _______________________________.

5 The cow lives in the _______________________________.

6 The monkey lives in the _______________________________.

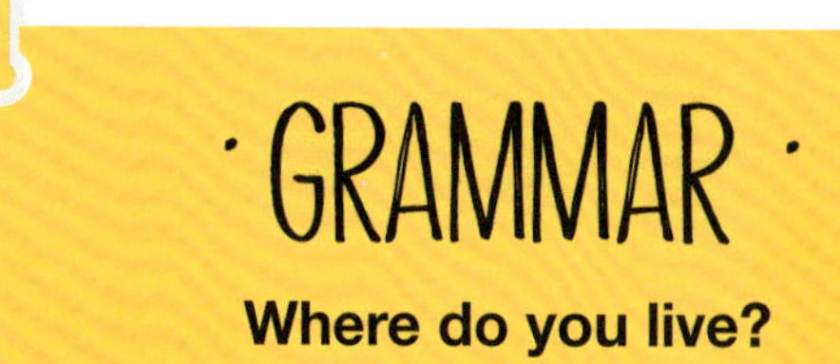

1 Listen, read, and say.

2 Sing and act. **Where Do You Live?**

Where do you live?	Where do you live?	Where do you live?
I live in the desert.	I live in the ocean.	I live in the city.
The desert! The desert!	The ocean! The ocean!	The city! The city!
The sizzling fizzling desert!	The splishy splashy ocean!	The busy whizzy city!

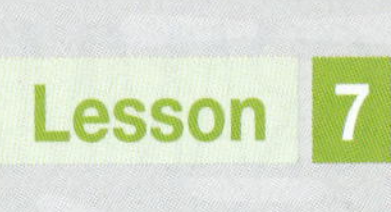

LET'S VISIT MONGOLIA

1 Read about home life in Mongolia.

Think Twice

1 Circle.

In Mongolia, a lot of people
live in yurts.   True / False

2 Complete about your country.

houses   boats   trailers
castles   apartments   tents

In ______________, a lot of people
live in ______________. Some people
live in ______________.

1 Draw, write, and say.

This is a tent
in Mongolia.

This is a / an _______________
in my country.

NEW FRIENDS

1 Complete the conversation. Choose your response.

I live in the country. Where do you live?

I live in the _______________.

Come and play at my house.

OK. Thank you! ◯   I'd love to. ◯

2 Act out the conversation.

·AUSTRALIA·

I like his music.
TRACK 66
Listen and circle the traditional music from Australia.
1 2 3 4

· VOCABULARY ·

TRACK 67

1 Listen, point, and say.

1 recorder

2 trumpet

3 drums

4 piano

5 violin

6 tambourine

TRACK 68

2 Listen and guess.

3 Act and say.

WORKBOOK
page 59

TRACK 69

1 Listen, read, and say.

2 Complete and circle.

1 Do you _________________________ the trumpet? Yes, I do. / No, I don't.

2 _________________________ play the drums? Yes, I do. / No, I don't.

3 Ask and answer.

the piano   the recorder   the violin
soccer   computer games   board games

WORKBOOK
page 60

GRAMMAR GUIDE
page 132

93

·SOUNDS GREAT·

  **TRACK 70**

1 Listen and chant.

Put on your coat,
Get in the boat,
Sit down low,
And row, row, row!

 **TRACK 71**

2 Listen, say, and color.

 **oa**    **ow**

boat

row

coat

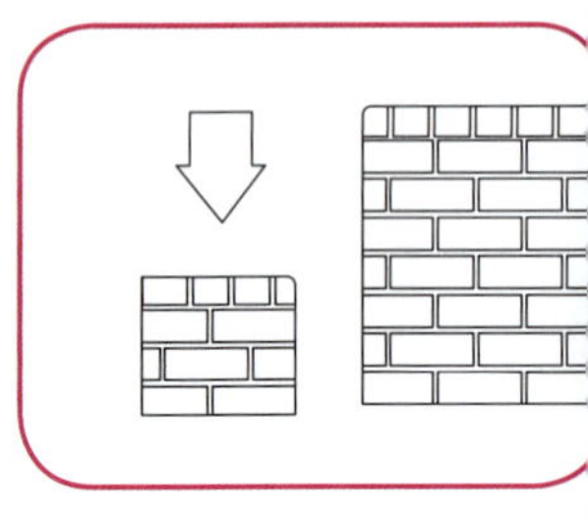

low

3 Look and write.

4 Read the chant and underline *oa* and *ow*.

WORKBOOK page 61

TRACK 72

1 Listen and read.

 **2** Read the story again. Check (✓) the **value** ⭐.

Play an instrument. ○   Help your friends. ○

 **3** How do you help your friends? Circle.

I help my friends to **play computer games** / **make models** / **climb trees** / **do homework** / **spell**.

TRACK 73

1 Listen, point, and say.

TRACK 74

2 Listen and say what's next.

TEMPLATE 8

3 Make a chart and say.

WORKBOOK
page 63

TRACK 75

1 Listen, read, and say.

TRACK 76

2 Sing and act. **Action Girl**

Does she play soccer on Mondays?
Does she play the trumpet on Tuesdays?
Yes, she does. Yes, she does.
She's an action girl.

Does she do taekwondo on Wednesdays?
Does she play the piano on Thursdays?
Yes, she does. Yes, she does.
She's an action girl.

Does she go to sleep on Fridays?
Does she go to sleep on Fridays?
Yes, she does. Yes, she does.
She's a very tired girl!

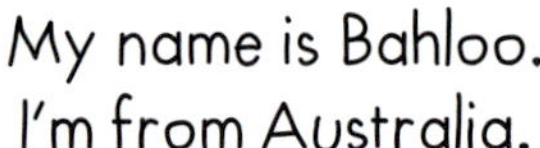

1 Read about a boy from Australia.

I like listening to and playing music. I'm a musician. I play the drums, the tambourine, and a special instrument called the didgeridoo. It's a traditional musical instrument from Australia.

After school, I play music on Mondays, Wednesdays, and Fridays. On Tuesdays and Thursdays, I draw pictures. On Saturdays and Sundays, I make models and I paint. I'm very creative!

Think Twice

1 What does Bahloo like doing? Circle.

painting / playing the drums / playing soccer / drawing / watching TV

2 Do you like music and art?

1 Draw, write, and say.

NEW FRIENDS

1 Complete the conversation. Choose your response.

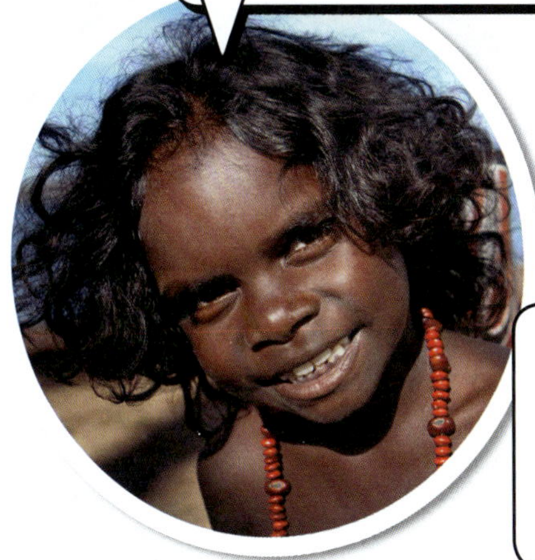

2 Act out the conversation.

1 Look, match, and write.

1 _________________________ in a cave.

2 _________________________ in a trailer.

3 _________________________ in a boat.

4 __He lives__________________ in a castle.

2 Look and complete. Then ask and answer.

THINK AGAIN!

A typical home in Mongolia is a _________________________.

My favorite lesson is on page _________________________.

An animal from Mongolia is _________________________.

WORKBOOK
page 66

STICKERS

PASSPORT
page 14

· PROGRESS CHECK ·

1 Write *Yes, I do.* or *No, I don't.*

1 Do you play the piano? ________________________.

2 Do you play the trumpet? ________________________.

3 Do you play the tambourine? ________________________.

4 Do you play the drums? ________________________.

5 Do you play the violin? ________________________.

6 Do you play the recorder? ________________________.

2 Look and write *Yes, he does.* or *No, he doesn't.*

1 Does he play the piano on Mondays? ________________________.

2 Does he play soccer on Thursdays? ________________________.

3 Does he play the trumpet on Fridays? ________________________.

4 Does he play with friends on Saturdays? ________________________.

5 Does he play the tambourine on Sundays? ________________________.

THINK AGAIN!

A traditional instrument from Australia is the ________________________.

My favorite picture is on page ________________________.

My favorite lesson is on page ________________________.

WORKBOOK
page 67

STICKERS

PASSPORT
page 16

STEAM

TEAM NAME

This is a traditional home in Mongolia called a *ger*.

The wood is painted with patterns.

Neighbors live next to each other.

Nomadic people move their home from place to place. Why do you think that is?

1 Get materials.

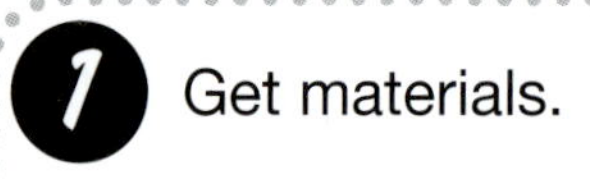

cardboard tube

mirrored sheet

markers

tape

tracing paper

scissors

straw

2 Draw three rectangles on the mirrored sheet. Cut them out.

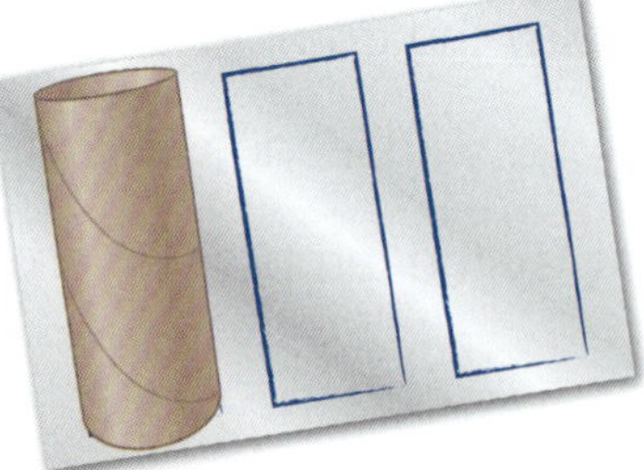

The patterns on the didgeridoo tell a story.

The patterns on the door are symbols of good wishes.

MAKE A KALEIDOSCOPE

AUSTRALIA

3 Tape and fold into a triangle.

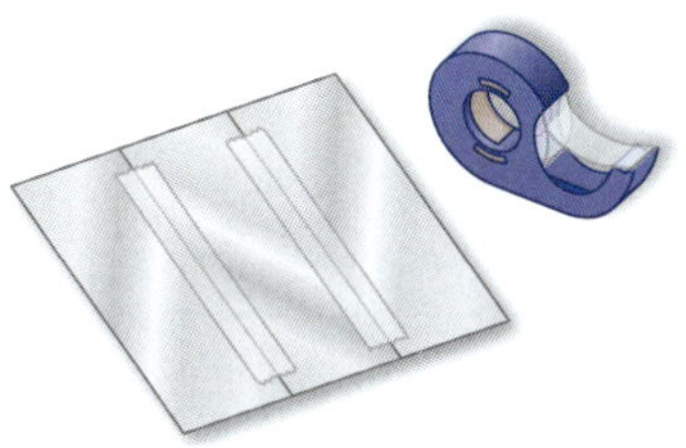

4 Put in tube.

5 Cut straw and tape to top.

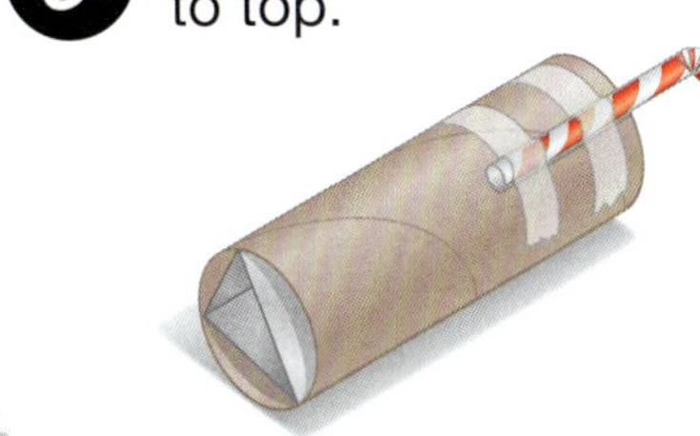

Aboriginal people paint stories using small circles or dots.

6 Decorate tracing paper with a pattern from Mongolia or Australia.

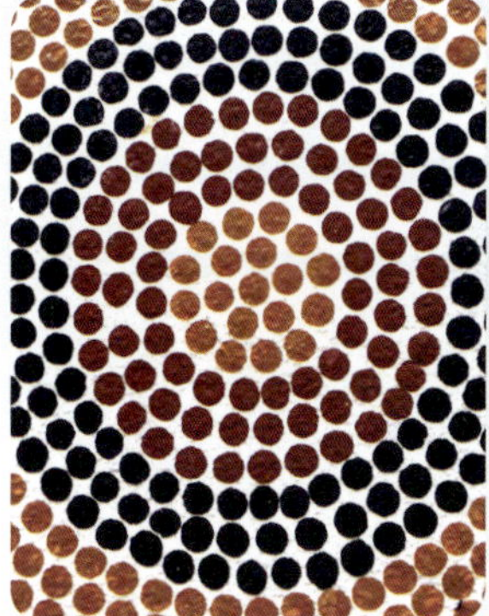

The dot designs fill the painting.

7 Attach pattern to straw. Look into the light!

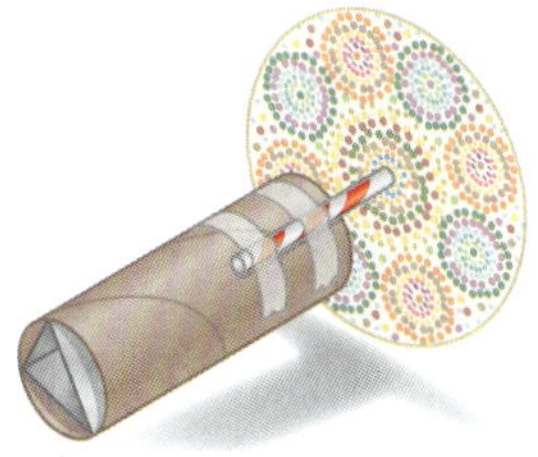

The colors come from nature.

Which patterns are traditional in your country?

THAILAND
WELCOME TO ★ WELCOME TO
Kingdom of
THAILAND
Pattaya
WELCOME TO ★ WELCOME TO
We're in Thailand!
Look at the flowers and fruit. They're on boats!
UNIT
9

Check (✓) three other types of transportation used in Thailand.
1
2
3
4

·VOCABULARY·

TRACK 77

1 Listen, point, and say.

1 airplane

2 bus

3 helicopter

4 car

5 train

6 motorcycle

TRACK 78

2 Listen and guess.

3 Play the Memory Game.

WORKBOOK
page 68

TRACK 79

1 Listen, read, and say.

· GRAMMAR ·

I don't go to school **by** train.
I go by bus.
He / She doesn't go to school **by** boat.
He / She goes by train.

2 Complete.

1 He _________________________ to school by bus.

He _________________________ by train.

2 She _________________________ to school by motorcycle.

She _________________________ by bus.

3 Talk to a friend.

WORKBOOK page 69

GRAMMAR GUIDE page 133

·SOUNDS GREAT·

TRACK 80

1 Listen and chant.

TRACK 81

2 Listen, say, and color.

blue

glue

new

3 Write and match.

bl _____ _____

gl _____ _____

n _____ _____

4 Read the chant and underline *ue* and *ew*.

·READING TIME·

TRACK 82

1 Listen and read.

 **2** Read the story again. Check (✔) the **value** ⭐.

Care for the environment. ◯   Walk to the beach. ◯

 **3** How do you go to the local store? Circle.

· VOCABULARY ·

TRACK 83

1 Listen, point, and say.

 ten

 twenty

 thirty

 forty

 fifty

sixty seventy eighty ninety one hundred

2 Match.

100   20   60   10   40   30

forty   twenty   one hundred   thirty   ten   sixty

T TEMPLATE 9

3 Complete, write, and say.

There are eighty bikes.

WORKBOOK page 72

TRACK 84

1 Listen, read, and say.

2 Ask and answer.

pencils   chairs   windows   desks

TRACK 85

3 Sing. **The Picnic Box**

How many apples are there in the picnic box?
There are forty and two,
That makes forty-two …

How many sandwiches are there in the picnic box?
There are twenty and six,
That makes twenty-six …

How many cookies are there in the picnic box?
There are thirty and five,
That makes thirty-five …

WORKBOOK page 73   GRAMMAR GUIDE page 133

LET'S VISIT THAILAND

1 Read about city life in Thailand.

Think Twice

1 Circle.

Mali goes to school by bus / taxi / tuk-tuk / river taxi.

2 Are there different kinds of taxis in your country?

·SPEAKING TIME·

1 Draw, write, and say.

NEW FRIENDS

1 Complete the conversation. Choose your response.

2 Act out the conversation.

·PERU·
WELCOME TO
PERU
INTERNATIONAL AIRPORT
TOURISM
Welcome to Peru!
I like her clothes. Look at the colors.
UNIT 10

Color the clothes to
match the photo.
1
2
3
4

Lesson 1

 TRACK 86

1 Listen, point, and say.

2 Read, color, and say.

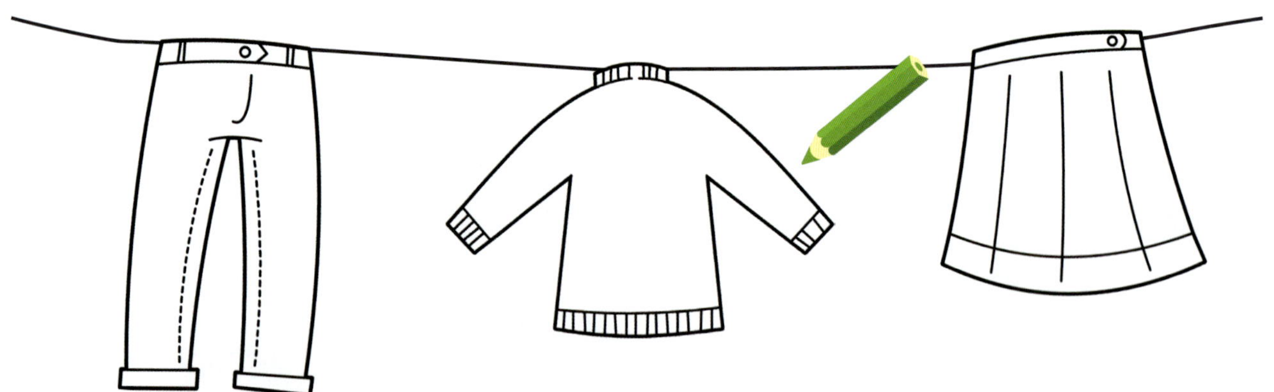

 **3** Find and circle.

o	b	v	g	m	y	u	z	l	p
s	n	e	a	k	e	r	s	i	a
h	f	m	k	t	c	j	h	p	n
o	q	b	i	x	s	k	i	r	t
e	l	p	y	a	c	m	r	o	s
s	w	b	s	w	e	a	t	e	r

WORKBOOK
page 75

TRACK 87

1 Listen, read, and say.

2 Look and write.

1 These are _________________ shoes.

2 This is _________________ shirt.

3 Find some things and say.

WORKBOOK
page 76

GRAMMAR
GUIDE
page 133

117

·SOUNDS GREAT·

TRACK 88

1 Listen and chant.

New clothes for your birthday.
From your mother and me.
Let's sing "Happy Birthday."
One, two, three …

TRACK 89

2 Listen, say, and color.

th **th**

three   birthday   mother   clothes

3 Write **th** or **th**.

mo ___ ___ er   ___ ___ ree   clo ___ ___ es   bir ___ ___ day

4 Read the chant and underline *th*.

TRACK 90

1 Listen and read.

1

2

3

4

2 Read the story again. Check (✓) the **value**⭐.

Say "Thank you." ◯   Share with family and friends. ◯

3 What do you share with your family? Circle.

clothes / books / candy / bedroom / toys

·VOCABULARY·

TRACK 91

1 Listen, point, and say.

2 Complete.

1 It's a _______________ skirt.

4 They're _______________ sneakers.

2 It's a _______________ shirt.

5 They're _______________ pants.

3 They're _______________ shoes.

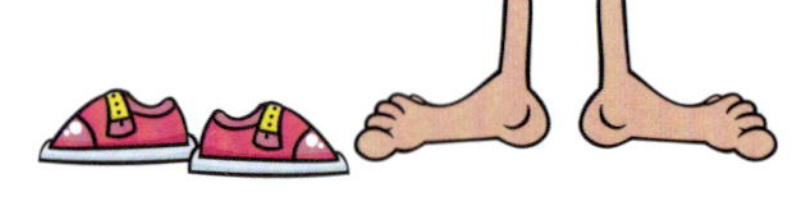

6 They're _______________ shoes.

3 Look and talk to a friend.

TRACK 92

1 Listen, read, and say.

2 Complete.

1 Bob _________________________ hat.

2 Alex _________________________ dog.

TRACK 93

TEMPLATE 10

3 Draw, color, and sing. **Our Clothes**

I have a new, new, new shirt.

She has an old, old, old skirt.

He has big, big, big sneakers.

I have small, small, small shoes.

We like our clothes!

We like our clothes!

LET'S VISIT PERU

1 Read about musical instruments from Peru.

Peru is famous for musical instruments. This is my musical instrument. It's called the pan pipes. The music is very beautiful. The pipes are short and long.

This is my sister. She plays a special guitar from Peru. It's very small, and it's old. My sister likes playing this guitar. She doesn't like playing big guitars. She can play the guitar and the pan pipes.

Think Twice

1 Circle.
Pedro can play the guitar and the pan pipes.   True / False

2 Do you like music?

1 Draw, write, and say.

NEW FRIENDS

1 Complete the conversation. Choose your response.

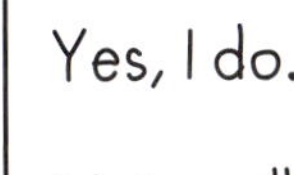

2 Act out the conversation.

1 Complete.

1 ___He doesn't go___ to school by motorcycle.
___He goes___ by bike.

2 _________________ to school by bus.
_________________ by car.

3 _________________ to school by helicopter.
_________________ by train.

4 _________________ to school by airplane.
_________________ by taxi.

2 Write. Then ask and answer.

1 20  + 7  = ___27 butterflies___

2 50  + 2  = _________________

3 70  + 1  = _________________

4 40 + 7 = _________________

THINK AGAIN!

A type of transportation in Thailand is _________________.

My favorite lesson is on page _________________.

A city in Thailand is _________________.

WORKBOOK page 82   **STICKERS**   **PASSPORT** page 18

·PROGRESS CHECK·

 **1** Complete and say.

1 Fiona has a ______ long skirt ______ .

2 Rosy has a ______________________ .

3 Fiona has an ______________________ .

4 Rosy has a ______________________ .

Fiona and Rosy.

 **2** Write.

This is

______ Fiona's skirt ______ .

This is

______________________ .

These are

______________________ .

This is

______________________ .

THINK AGAIN!

A musical instrument from Peru is ______________________ .

My favorite picture is on page ______________________ .

Clothes people wear in Peru are ______________________ .

Paknam temple and Khlong-Dan river, Bangkok.

Amphawa floating market, Bangkok.

The boats in the floating market are small and made of wood.

STEAM

TEAM NAME

Make predictions about objects that will float or sink.

float	sink

1 Select the materials you need to design your boat.

Many Thai boats are decorated with colored ribbons and flowers to pay respect to water spirits.

Some Uru boats have a feline figurehead on the bow. The puma is a sacred animal for the Andean peoples.

· FLOAT YOUR BOAT·

PERU

2 Design and build a boat. Look at some examples.

3 Test your boat. Does it sink or float?

____

4 Add coins to your boat. Does it sink or float?

____

5 Draw your boat.

What makes the water a good or a bad place to live?

The Uru people live on the islands of Lake Titicaca.

The islands are made of reeds.

Balsas are boats made of dried reeds.

TEAMWORK ★ ★ ★ ★ ★

HOW TO USE THE GRAMMAR GUIDE

GRANT'S HOME STUDY GUIDE

1 Read your grammar guide again at home.

2 Look at the example. Close your book. Try to say the example.

3 Open your book and check.

1 After your grammar lessons, turn to the Grammar Guide. Look at the example.

Sit down, please.
Don't talk.

2 Complete the activity.

Complete. 

1 Stand ___up___, please.

2 Don't sit ________.

3 Clean up, ________.

4 ________ shout.

3 Check your answers.

CANADA

GERMANY

Complete.

1 Stand _____________, please.

2 Don't sit _____________.

3 Clean up, _____________.

4 _____________ shout.

Complete.

1 What _________ is it? It's three

_______________.

2 _________ _________ is it? _________
two o'clock.

3 What time _________ _________?

_________ five _______________.

Complete.

1 How _________ you spell "snake"?

2 _________ do you _________ "panda"?

3 _________ _________ you spell "clock"?

4 _________ do you _________ your

name? _____________

Complete.

1 I get _________ at _________ o'clock.

2 I have lunch at _________

_______________.

3 I _________ dinner at _________

_______________ in the evening.

4 I go to bed _________ _________
o'clock at night.

UNIT 3 KENYA

Complete.

1 That's _________ chicken.

2 This _________ _________ sheep.

3 Those _________ birds.

4 These _________ ducks.

Complete.

1 _________ that?

2 _________ _________ ant.

3 What _________ those?

4 _________ grasshoppers.

UNIT 4 TURKEY

Complete.

1 _________ you like onions? Yes, I _________.

2 Do you _________ beans? _________, I do.

3 Do _________ like ants? No, I _________.

4 Do you like _________? _________, I don't.

Complete.

1 I _________ carrots.

2 I _________ pancakes.

3 I _________ peppers.

4 I _________ cookies.

5 SOUTH KOREA

6 ARGENTINA

Complete.

1 __________ you play the guitar?

__________, I can.

2 Can __________ jump rope? No, I

__________.

3 Can you touch your toes?

__________.

4 Can you climb a tree?

__________.

Complete.

1 Dogs __________ sing.

2 Birds __________ sing.

3 Dogs __________ fly.

4 Birds __________ fly.

Complete.

1 What __________ you like __________?

2 I __________ reading.

3 I __________ like playing soccer.

4 I __________.

Complete. Write about your friend.

1 He / She likes __________.

2 He / She doesn't like __________.

3 He / She __________.

MONGOLIA

AUSTRALIA

Lesson 2

He / She / It lives in a house boat.

Write the words in order.

1 She castle lives a in

_______________________________________.

2 trailer a in He lives

_______________________________________.

3 in lives cave It a

_______________________________________.

Lesson 2

Do you play the guitar?
Yes, **I do.** /
No, **I don't.**

Complete.

1 __________ you play the violin? Yes, I

__________.

2 Do __________ play the piano?

__________, I don't.

3 __________ you __________ soccer?

__________, __________ do.

Lesson 6

Where do you live?
I live in the country.

Complete.

1 __________ do you live?

2 I __________ in the city.

3 Where __________ you __________?

4 I live __________ __________ jungle.

Lesson 6

Does he / she play soccer **on** Tuesdays?
Yes, **he / she does.**
No, **he / she doesn't.**

Complete.

1 __________ he go to the park on

Tuesdays? __________, he doesn't.

2 Does __________ play soccer __________

Mondays? Yes, he __________.

3 __________ he __________ to the mall

__________ Thursdays? No, __________

__________.

UNIT 9 THAILAND

Lesson 2

I don't go to school **by** train.
I go by bus.
He / She doesn't go to school **by** bus.
He / She goes by bike.

Complete.

1 _________ doesn't go to school by train. He _________ by bus.

2 She _________ go to school _________ bike. _________ goes _________ bus.

3 I don't _________________.
I _________________.

Lesson 6

How many pencils **are there**?
There are twenty-four.

Complete.

1 How many apples are _________?
_________ are eight.

2 _________ many bananas _________ there? There _________ four.

3 _________ cookies are there? _________ _________ ten.

UNIT 10 PERU

Lesson 2

This is Maria's backpack.
These are Maria's books.

Complete.

1 This _________ Maria's skirt.

2 _________ are Tom's books.

3 _________ is Alan's shirt.

4 These _________ Grant's sneakers.

Lesson 6

He / She has an old guitar.

Write the words in order.

1 He big has hat a
_________________.

2 has short He pants
_________________.

3 new has sneakers He
_________________.

Getty Images, graphixel/iStockphoto/Getty Images, florin1961/iStockphoto/Getty Images, Anadolu Agency/Getty Images; p. 56: pius99/iStockphoto/Getty Images; p. 62: marcutti/iStockphoto/Getty Images, hanapon1002/iStockphoto/Getty Images, LumineImages/iStockphoto/Getty Images, PeopleImages/iStockphoto/Getty Images, SerrNovik/iStockphoto/Getty Images, Trout55/iStockphoto/Getty Images; p. 64: Sirikornt/iStockphoto/Getty Images, ma-no/iStockphoto/Getty Images, Alamy/Fotoarena; p. 65: Carl Court/Getty Images; p. 66: holgs/iStockphoto/Getty Images; p. 67: Alamy/Fotoarena, Gerville/iStockphoto/Getty Images, ozgurdonmaz/iStockphoto/Getty Images, Alamy/Fotoarena; p. 68: szirtesi/iStockphoto/Getty Images, AndreyPopov/iStockphoto/Getty Images, Neustockimages/iStockphoto/Getty Images, iofoto/iStockphoto/Getty Images, Wavebreakmedia/iStockphoto/Getty Images, nd3000/iStockphoto/Getty Images, Tolikoff Photography/iStockphoto/Getty Images, DragonImages/iStockphoto/Getty Images, arekmalang/iStockphoto/Getty Images; p. 74: Choreograph/iStockphoto/Getty Images, yacobchuk/iStockphoto/Getty Images; p. 78: liangpv/iStockphoto/Getty Images, Im Yeongsik/iStockphoto/Getty Images, valentinrussanov/iStockphoto/Getty Images, vanbeets/iStockphoto/Getty Images, TwilightShow/iStockphoto/Getty Images, Ziva_K/iStockphoto/Getty Images, deepblue4you/iStockphoto/Getty Images, Eduard Lysenko/iStockphoto/Getty Images, Marco Tulio/iStockphoto/Getty Images, RusN/iStockphoto/Getty Images, Phawintphat/iStockphoto/Getty Images, chromatos/iStockphoto/Getty Images, tttuna/iStockphoto/Getty Images, malerapaso/iStockphoto/Getty Images, svrid79/iStockphoto/Getty Images, pius99/iStockphoto/Getty Images; p. 79: diverroy/iStockphoto/Getty Images, piccaya/iStockphoto/Getty Images, piccaya/iStockphoto/Getty Images, Alamy/Fotoarena; p. 80: Lucy Brown/iStockphoto/Getty Images, Goddard_Photography/iStockphoto/Getty Images, namibelephant/iStockphoto/Getty Images, Windofchange64/iStockphoto/Getty Images, afhunta/iStockphoto/Getty Images; p. 86: DarrenMower/iStockphoto/Getty Images, VSFP/iStockphoto/Getty Images, hectojcm/iStockphoto/Getty Images, LuCaAr/iStockphoto/Getty Images, scaliger/iStockphoto/Getty Images, RuudMorijn/iStockphoto/Getty Images; p. 88: Rawpixel/iStockphoto/Getty Images, Tuul & Bruno Morandi/Getty Images, withgod/iStockphoto/Getty Images; p. 89: molloykeith/iStockphoto/Getty Images; p. 90: Ida Jarosova/iStockphoto/Getty Images; p. 92: Bronwyn8/iStockphoto/Getty Images, istudio5/iStockphoto/Getty Images, ajkkafe/iStockphoto/Getty Images, Wavebreakmedia/iStockphoto/Getty Images, Wavebreakmedia/iStockphoto/Getty Images, Martinan/iStockphoto/Getty Images; p. 98: Lonely Planet Images/Getty Images, Violetastock/iStockphoto/Getty Images, Paul Patton/iStockphoto/Getty Images; p. 102: Panya-/iStockphoto/Getty Images, Bartosz Hadyniak/iStockphoto/Getty Images, bizoo_n/iStockphoto/Getty Images, gionnixxx/iStockphoto/Getty Images, zelg/iStockphoto/Getty Images,UIG/Glow Images, Beto Celli, Lemon_tm/iStockphoto/Getty Images, letoosen/iStockphoto/Getty Images, chromatos/iStockphoto/Getty Images, Coprid/iStockphoto/Getty Images, Michael Burrell/iStockphoto/Getty Images, Eduard Lysenko/iStockphoto/Getty Images, koya79/iStockphoto/Getty Images; p. 103: bodrumsurf/iStockphoto/Getty Images, Photoresearchers/Latinstock, kira_an/iStockphoto/Getty Images, Lonely Planet Images/iStockphoto/Getty Images, kira_an/iStockphoto/Getty Images; p. 104: nimon_t/iStockphoto/Getty Images; p. 105: tbradford/iStockphoto/Getty Images, Halfpoint/iStockphoto/Getty Images, ayaka_photo/iStockphoto/Getty Images, olaser/iStockphoto/Getty Images; p. 106: Travellinglight/iStockphoto/Getty Images, mladn61/iStockphoto/Getty Images, Balefire9/iStockphoto/Getty Images, Tramino/iStockphoto/Getty Images, sculpies/iStockphoto/Getty Images, Ljupco/iStockphoto/Getty Images; p. 112: pat138241/iStockphoto/Getty Images, intek1/iStockphoto/Getty Images, Leonardo Monteverde/iStockphoto/Getty Images; p. 114: Bartosz Hadyniak/iStockphoto/Getty Images; p. 116: GaryAlvis/iStockphoto/Getty Images, kunchit2512/iStockphoto/Getty Images, popovaphoto/iStockphoto/Getty Images, NYS444/iStockphoto/Getty Images, popovaphoto/iStockphoto/Getty Images, PaulPaladin/iStockphoto/Getty Images; p. 122: hadynyah/iStockphoto/Getty Images, cuklom/iStockphoto/Getty Images, Jose Girarte/iStockphoto/Getty Images; p. 126: liangpv/iStockphoto/Getty Images, NicolasMcComber/iStockphoto/Getty Images, Photoprofi30/iStockphoto/Getty Images, enviromantic/iStockphoto/Getty Images,letty17/iStockphoto/Getty Images,viviamo/iStockphoto/Getty Images, izusek/iStockphoto/Getty Images,RTimages/iStockphoto/Getty Images, vuk8691/iStockphoto/Getty Images, Uwe-Bergwitz/iStockphoto/Getty Images, photka/iStockphoto/Getty Images, imon_t/iStockphoto/Getty Images; p. 127: VanReeel/iStockphoto/Getty Images, hadynyah/iStockphoto/Getty Images, 1001nights/iStockphoto/Getty Images, traveler1116/iStockphoto/Getty Images.

Dados Internacionais de Catalogação na Publicação (CIP)

Bibliotecária responsável: Aline Graziele Benitez CRB-1/3129

C23n Cant, Amanda

1.ed.　　Next Station 2: Student's Book / Amanda Cant, Mary Charrington, Sarah Elizabeth Sprague; [Adapt.] Viv Lambert. – 1.ed. – São Paulo: Macmillan Education do Brasil, 2020.

136 p.; il.; 21 x 27 cm. – (Coleção Next Station)

ISBN: 978-85-511-0128-5

1. Língua inglesa. I. Charrington, Mary. II. Sprague, Sarah Elizabeth. III. Lambert, Viv. IV. Título. V. Série.

CDD 420

Índice para catálogo sistemático:

1. Língua inglesa

MACMILLAN EDUCATION DO BRASIL
Av. Brigadeiro Faria Lima, 1.309, 3° Andar –
Jd. Paulistano – São Paulo – SP – 01452-002
www.macmillan.com.br
Customer Service: [55] (11) 4613-2278
0800 16 88 77
Fax: [55] (11) 4612-6098

Printed in Brazil. Pancrom 10/2023

·MAP STICKERS·

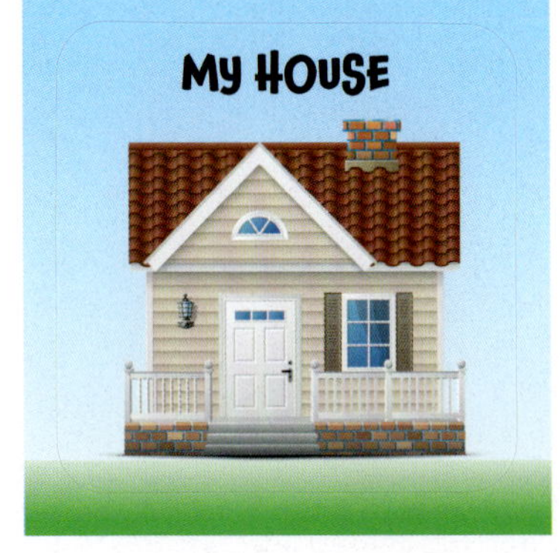

·PASSPORT STICKERS·

WELCOME TO
SOUTH KOREA
WELCOME TO

ARRIVAL
GERMANY
18 AUG
BERLIN AIRPORT

Türkiye Cumhuriyeti
TURKEY
Republic of Turkey

WELCOME TO
PERU
INTERNATIONAL AIRPORT
TOURISM

CONTROL
DEPARTURE
ARGENTINA
25 JULY
approved

WELCOME TO
CANADA
TORONTO AIRPORT
(TIME 05:00 AM)
(MAX: 699)
08 APR
ARRVL.

WELCOME TO
MONGOLIA
INTERNATIONAL AIRPORT
TOURISM
23 · SEPT

WELCOME TO SYDNEY
< ARRIVAL >
AUSTRALIA
IMMIGRATION CONTROL
15 SEPT
PERMITTED TO ENTER AND STAY FOR 30 DAYS

24 NOV
KENYA
NAIROBI
INTERNATIONAL
AIRPORT

WELCOME TO · WELCOME TO
Kingdom of
THAILAND
Pattaya
WELCOME TO · WELCOME TO